SERIES TITLES

This Zak Books edition was published in 2009.
Zak Books is an imprint of McRae Books.

LATE MEDIEVAL EUROPE

was created and produced by McRae Books Srl
Via del Salviatino, 1 — 50016 — Fiesole
(Florence), (Italy)
info@mcraebooks.com
www.mcraebooks.com

Publishers: Anne McRae, Marco Nardi
Series Editor: Anne McRae
Author: Neil Morris
Main Illustrations: Giorgio Bacchin pp. 10–1;
Emmanuelle Etienne pp. 32–33; Inklink pp. 18–19;
Lucia Mattioli pp. 30–31; Alessandro Menchi pp.
44–45; MM comunicazione (M. Cappon, M. Favilli,G.
Sbragi, C. Scutti) pp. 12–13, 15, 25, 43; Tiziano
Perotto 16–17, 22–23, 28; Sergio pp. 35, 41
Illustrations: Studio Stalio (Alessandro
Cantucci, Fabiano Fabbrucci)
Maps: M. Paola Baldanzi
Photos: By permission of the British Library,
Add. MS 14761, p.37; Bridgeman Art
Library, London/ Archivi Alinari, Florence p.
91; Scala Archives, Florence pp. 6–7t, 21b,
38–39b;
Art Director: Marco Nardi
Layouts: Starry Dog Books Ltd.
Project Editor: Loredana Agosta
Research: Loredana Agosta
Editing: Tall Tree Ltd., London
Repro: Litocolor, Florence

Consultant:
Dr. Norman Housley was born in Trowbridge,
Wiltshire, in 1952. He has studied the history of
the Middle Ages for 30 years and has taught at the
University of Leicester since 1983. He has written
or edited ten books and numerous specialist articles
about the Crusades.

Library of Congress Cataloging-in-Publication Data

Morris, Neil, 1946-
  Late medieval Europe / Neil Morris.
      p. cm. -- (History of the world ; 9)
  Includes index.
  Summary: "A detailed overview of the history of
medieval Europe from about 1000 to 1500"--Provided
by publisher.
  ISBN 978-8860981523
  1. Middle Ages--Juvenile literature. 2. Europe--
History--476-1492--Juvenile literature. 3. Civilization,
Medieval--Juvenile literature. I. Title.
  D200.M67 2009
  910.1'7--dc22
                                                2008008407

Printed and bound in Malaysia.

Late Medieval Europe

Neil Morris

Consultant: Dr Norman Housley, Professor of History, University of Leicester

Zak
BOOKS

Contents

Hunting with falcons was a popular pastime with Medieval nobles, who developed the sport as part of their courtly culture.

TIMELINE

	1050 CE	1100	1150	1200	1200
THE CRUSADES		First Crusade leads to the capture of Jerusalem and creation of Crusader states.	Second Crusade—Muslim forces victorious in Damascus.	Third Crusade.	Fourth Crusade. Fifth Crusade. Sixth Crusade.
ITALY	Normans invade Sicily.			Holy Roman Emperor Frederick II rules Sicily.	
ENGLAND AND FRANCE			Henry II becomes King of England.	King John seals the Magna Carta. Philip II is ruler of northern France and Flanders.	
HOLY ROMAN EMPIRE			Conrad III joins the Second Crusade.	Frederick I dies on the Third Crusade to the Holy Land.	
SPAIN		Alfonso VI of Castile and León recaptures Toledo from the Moors.		The Muslim Almohads are defeated at the Battle of Las Navas de Tolosa.	
THE CHURCH AND THE PAPACY		Pope Gregory VII claims power over all Europe's leaders.	Cistercian order of monks founded at Citeaux in France.		
EASTERN EUROPE			Vladimir II rules as Grand Prince of Kiev.	Order of Teutonic Knights is founded in Acre.	Mongols from the east cross the frozen Volga River.

Introduction

This book covers approximately five centuries of European history, starting around the year 1000. Great changes occurred throughout the continent during this period of the later Middle Ages. The population increased as towns and cities grew, new kingdoms were formed, and violent battles were fought for power and land. Kings and nobles built castles, while the Church constructed magnificent cathedrals, and throughout much of the period, there was conflict between Church and State. Invaders came from other continents—Moors from Africa and Mongols from Asia—and a deadly disease, the Black Death, killed millions. Important advances were made in technology and learning, as the arts and sciences developed towards the inspired flowering of the Renaissance.

During the Middle Ages, developments in trade and banking led to the growth of cities, such as Florence in Italy.

The basinet helmet had a hinged visor to cover a knight's face. Armed warfare was a Medieval knight's way of life.

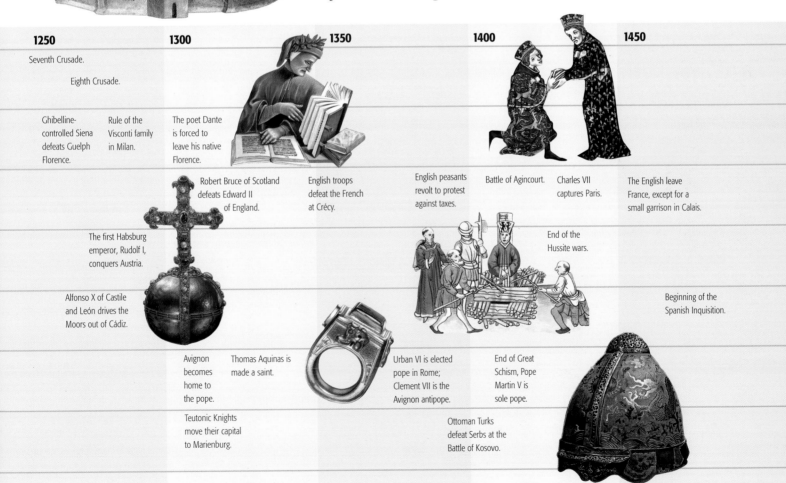

1250	1300	1350	1400	1450
Seventh Crusade.				
Eighth Crusade.				
Ghibelline-controlled Siena defeats Guelph Florence.	Rule of the Visconti family in Milan.	The poet Dante is forced to leave his native Florence.		
	Robert Bruce of Scotland defeats Edward II of England.	English troops defeat the French at Crécy.	English peasants revolt to protest against taxes.	Battle of Agincourt. Charles VII captures Paris.	The English leave France, except for a small garrison in Calais.
The first Habsburg emperor, Rudolf I, conquers Austria.				End of the Hussite wars.
Alfonso X of Castile and León drives the Moors out of Cádiz.				Beginning of the Spanish Inquisition.
	Avignon becomes home to the pope.	Thomas Aquinas is made a saint.	Urban VI is elected pope in Rome; Clement VII is the Avignon antipope.	End of Great Schism, Pope Martin V is sole pope.
	Teutonic Knights move their capital to Marienburg.		Ottoman Turks defeat Serbs at the Battle of Kosovo.	

Europe from the Year 1000

There were great advances in learning, agriculture, and trade in Europe during the first centuries of the new millennium. The first universities opened and new monastic orders were founded, and Christian beliefs dominated society. Though peasant farmers were no longer slaves, they were not free either. However, life for ordinary people gradually improved.

A 12th-century mosaic in Monreale Cathedral, Sicily, showing the creation of the stars.

View of the World

Medieval thinkers believed that the Earth was the center of the Universe, with the stars and planets moving around it. As Christians, they also believed that God created the world. Thinkers and theologians, such as Thomas Aquinas, brought Christian faith and human reason together.

Knowledge

Astronomers used astrolabes and other instruments to learn more about the stars and planets. People believed that these celestial bodies directly affected their lives. This meant that astrologers were also important, since they used astronomical calculations to interpret earthly events.

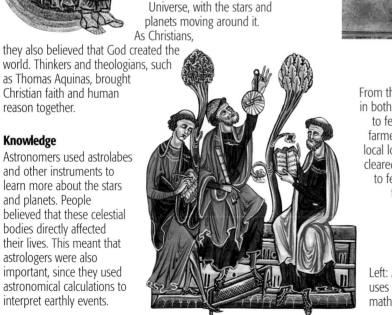

The Recovery of Europe

From the 11th century great improvements in both farming methods and trade helped to feed the growing population. Peasant farmers, known as serfs, worked for their local lord, who owned land that had been cleared for agriculture. Serfs were allowed to feed their families from strips of land that they worked in the lord's fields.

A serf cuts and gathers wheat.

Left: A 13th-century astronomer (center) uses an astrolabe, accompanied by a mathematician (right) and a clerk (left).

AFTER YEAR 1000

1054
Split between western Catholic Church of Rome and Eastern Orthodox Church of Byzantium.

1084
Carthusian order of monks founded by St. Bruno of Cologne (c. 1030–1101) at Chartreuse in France.

c. 1088
First university founded at Bologna, Italy.

1098
Cistercian order of monks founded by St. Robert of Molesme (c. 1027–1110) at Citeaux in France.

c. 1170
Oxford University founded in England.

1211
The University of Paris (founded c. 1150) is recognized as a legal corporation.

c. 1225–1274
Life of Thomas Aquinas, who studied at the University of Naples and became professor of theology in Paris.

In this fresco by Andrea di Bonaiuti (c. 1343–1377), human figures of the liberal arts sit above Greek and Roman scholars.

The Liberal Arts
Knowledge was divided into seven subjects, based on ancient Greek and Roman learning, together known as the liberal arts. The first group of three subjects (or *trivium*) was made up of grammar, rhetoric, and logic. The second group of four (or *quadrivium*) consisted of arithmetic, astronomy, geometry, and music. Latin was the language of learning.

Universities
Early universities were founded at Bologna in Italy, Paris in France, and Oxford in England. They came about as groups of students organized themselves into corporations and employed scholars to teach them. After completing their studies in the liberal arts, students went on to study law, medicine, and theology.

A scholar teaching at the University of Paris.

Feudal Society

Under the Medieval feudal system, noblemen had control over their own lands. They had the power to collect taxes, settle legal disputes, and keep their own army of knights. As the ruling class in Europe, they were subject only to the king. At the same time, the clergy represented the considerable power of the Church, and they also collected taxes from those who did all the hard work—the peasants, or serfs.

Feudalism

Feudalism was the main social system in Medieval Europe. Kings leased lands to their nobles, or lords, in exchange for an oath of loyalty and military service when needed. In turn, the noblemen required the service of knights, who swore loyal oaths and were trained to fight for their lord and the king.

Lords and Vassals

Before a lord granted someone a fief, or land estate, he made him a vassal. He did this at a special ceremony, during which the vassal made oaths of homage and loyalty. The vassal promised to fight for his lord and also to advise him when he was faced with a major decision. If a lord was uncertain whether he should go to war, he held a council of all his vassals.

An 11th-century ivory chess piece in the form of a mounted warrior.

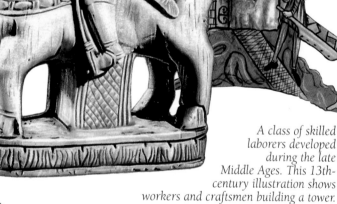

A class of skilled laborers developed during the late Middle Ages. This 13th-century illustration shows workers and craftsmen building a tower.

The Three Estates

The feudal structure meant that Medieval society was divided into three estates, or orders. This was summed up by an 11th-century bishop, who wrote that "some pray, others fight, still others work." The first group was made up of the clergy, who at local level were represented by the village priest. The nobility made up the second order, and they could raise troops and even fight themselves. The third group was made up of working peasants.

Left: The three estates: from the top, nobles, clergymen, and peasants.

Serfs, or peasant farmers, work the land for their local lord of the manor.

An illustration of Fortune turning her wheel. The king is on the top and the peasants are below.

Fortune

People believed in the idea of fortune, or chance, since they were convinced that earthly power did not last. This applied particularly to nobles, many of whom were seen as being sinfully ambitious. In illustrations, Fortune was represented as female, and she often turned a wheel, moving people up and down at her whim.

Peasant Workers

The peasants of the lowest estate made up the majority of the population. They had to work hard, and the products of their labor belonged to the lord of the manor. Before they fed themselves, they had to farm the lord's personal land to provide him and his family with food. Peasants also had to pay a tithe—a tenth of their produce—to the Church.

Illustration of the month of October from a prayer book owned by the Duc de Berry (1340–1416), an important French nobleman. It shows peasants tilling the land and sowing in the shadow of a palace.

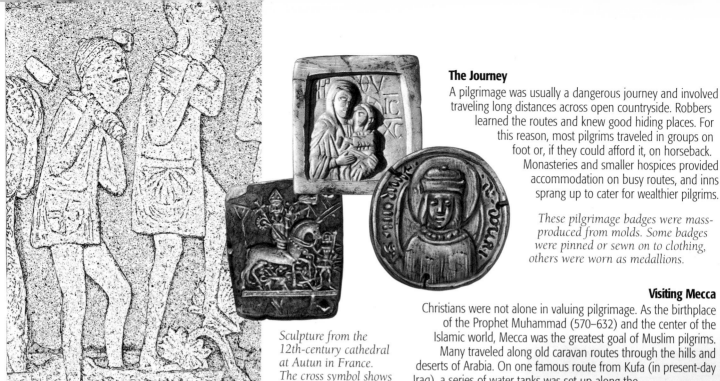

The Journey

A pilgrimage was usually a dangerous journey and involved traveling long distances across open countryside. Robbers learned the routes and knew good hiding places. For this reason, most pilgrims traveled in groups on foot or, if they could afford it, on horseback. Monasteries and smaller hospices provided accommodation on busy routes, and inns sprang up to cater for wealthier pilgrims.

These pilgrimage badges were mass-produced from molds. Some badges were pinned or sewn on to clothing, others were worn as medallions.

Sculpture from the 12th-century cathedral at Autun in France. The cross symbol shows that one pilgrim has visited Jerusalem. The shell refers to Santiago de Compostela.

Visiting Mecca

Christians were not alone in valuing pilgrimage. As the birthplace of the Prophet Muhammad (570–632) and the center of the Islamic world, Mecca was the greatest goal of Muslim pilgrims. Many traveled along old caravan routes through the hills and deserts of Arabia. On one famous route from Kufa (in present-day Iraq), a series of water tanks was set up along the route. The pilgrimage to Mecca, called the *hajj*, became a special duty for all Muslims able to make the journey.

Pilgrimage

Pilgrims went on long journeys to holy places and shrines. The most famous pilgrimage cities were Jerusalem, Rome, and Santiago de Compostela. Christians wanted to visit these places to show their religious devotion. Some pilgrims undertook their journey as an act of penance, hoping for forgiveness. Others went in order to pray for a miracle at their chosen holy site.

Muslim pilgrims on camels.

The Holy Land

The greatest aim of Christian pilgrims was to visit Jerusalem, where many events in the life of Jesus Christ (died c. 30) took place. For most, this involved an extremely hazardous journey because the region had been under Muslim rule for centuries. Christians' wish to be able to visit the Holy Land freely led to the military expeditions of the Crusades. Jerusalem was, and still is, also holy to Muslims and Jews.

An illustration of the walled city of Jerusalem from the 15th century.

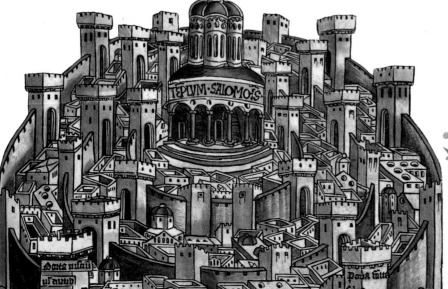

Gold-plated, bejeweled reliquary of St Foy, a young girl who was martyred in the 4th century. It contains the saint's skull.

ROUTES FROM FRANCE TO SANTIAGO DE COMPOSTELA

France

Spain

Main pilgrimage routes to Santiago de Compostela

Some sites on the route

ATLANTIC OCEAN

PARIS

TOURS

VÉZELAY

AUTUN

LE PUY

CONQUES

ARLES

TOULOUSE

SANTIAGO DE COMPOSTELA

LEÓN

BURGOS

PAMPLONA

MEDITERRANEAN SEA

Relics of the Saints

Christian pilgrims had a great wish to see and even touch holy places and objects associated with the lives of saints. They believed that bones of the apostle St. James (died 44 CE) had been taken to Compostela in Spain and were held in the cathedral there (Santiago means "St. James"). Bones and other items connected to the saints were called relics and were kept in containers called reliquaries.

Routes to Santiago de Compostela

The main pilgrimage routes through France and Spain led eventually to Santiago de Compostela. On their way to the northwest tip of Spain, pilgrims visited many churches that were famous for their relics, such as those in Tours and Toulouse. These churches had wide aisles that allowed pilgrims to pass and see shrines and relics easily.

Pilgrims flocked to the Abbey of St Foy at Conques in southern France. Many were on the long journey to Compostela.

The Crusades

From the late 11th to the 13th century, European Christians made a series of military expeditions to the lands of the eastern Mediterranean. The aim of these expeditions—the Crusades—was to free Jerusalem and the rest of the Holy Land from Muslim control. Battles were won and lost, but the Crusaders failed to gain lasting control over the region.

Pope Urban II on his way to Clermont.

"God Wills It"

In 1095, Byzantine emperor Alexius I Comnenus (reigned 1081–1118) asked Pope Urban II (reigned 1088–1099) for help in fighting the Muslim Turks. The pope held a council at Clermont in France, where he made a rousing speech. He called upon men of courage to help the Eastern Orthodox Church and to fight for the freedom of Jerusalem. His passionate call to arms was greeted with cries of "God wills it!"

Christian Knights

The main Crusader armies were made up of well-trained knights. They were men who had been dubbed knights by their lord at a solemn ceremony. When a knight vowed to go on Crusade, he went through another ceremony. The Crusade leader sewed a cloth cross to his clothing, as a symbol of God's protection.

The Crusaders recovered many Christian relics, such as this reliquary of the True Cross (the cross on which Jesus died).

An English knight leaves for a Crusade, seen off by his wife and daughter-in-law.

Preparing for Battle

The clergy assured Crusader knights that if they were killed doing God's work all their sins would be forgiven. Knights were also given practical privileges by the Church. Their possessions were protected while they were away, no debts were called in and no taxes collected. Well equipped with weapons and armor, the Crusaders were ready to fight for their Christian beliefs.

In this 14th century illustration, a knight receives his sword from the king.

Crusading Fervor

Many ordinary people felt inspired to help the cause. The so-called Peasants' Crusade of 1095–1099 was led by a Frenchman known as Peter the Hermit (c. 1050–1115). Most of his untrained rabble were massacred by the Turks. In 1212, thousands of boys and girls joined a Children's Crusade that set off from the Rhineland. Many starved, some were drowned in the Mediterranean Sea and others were sold into slavery.

CRUSADE ROUTES

By Land and Sea
Various routes took Crusaders all around the northern and eastern shores of the Mediterranean, as well as across it by sea. The military journeys also had the effect of opening up trade routes for Europeans, who replaced Byzantines and Muslims as merchants in the eastern Mediterranean.

SCOTLAND
IRELAND
DENMARK
ENGLAND
HOLY
DARTMOUTH
BOULOGNE COLOGNE
POLAND
BAYEUX ROUEN
ROMAN
ATLANTIC
PARIS
RATISBON (REGENSBURG)
OCEAN
Rhine
FRANCE
EMPIRE
HUNGARY
CLERMONT LYON
TOULOUSE
LEÓN AND
VENICE
CASTILE
MARSEILLE
BLACK SEA
SPALATO (SPLIT)
LISBON
ROME
RAGUSA
CONSTANTINOPLE (ISTANBUL)
(DUBROVNIK)
NAPLES BARI
BYZANTINE
ALEPPO
EMPIRE
(HALAB)
TUNIS
MESSINA
ANTIOCH
DAMASCUS
MEDITERRANEAN SEA
ACRE
JERUSALEM
DAMIETTA

Crusader states (1099–1144)
First Crusade
Second Crusade
Third Crusade
Fourth Crusade
Fifth Crusade
Political borders

THE CRUSADES

1096–1099
First Crusade leads to the capture of Jerusalem and creation of Crusader states.

1147–1149
Second Crusade—Muslim forces victorious in Damascus.

1189–1192
Third Crusade—despite loss of Jerusalem, Christian pilgrims are allowed free access.

1202–1204
Fourth Crusade leads to the sacking of Constantinople.

1217–1221
Fifth Crusade—capture of Damietta in Egypt.

1228–1229
Sixth Crusade leads to a peace treaty with the Muslim sultan.

1248–1254
Seventh Crusade— Muslims hold King Louis IX of France (reigned 1226–1270) to ransom.

1270–1272
Eighth Crusade—Crusaders land at Tunis, where Louis IX dies.

A large group of children leave for the Holy Land. None reached their destination.

Crusader States

After the success of the First Crusade, the Christian conquerors divided their territory into four states. The most important was the Kingdom of Jerusalem, on which the three states to the north—the Principality of Antioch and the Counties of Edessa and Tripoli—were dependent. Muslim forces gradually won back territory, but European presence in the region lasted for nearly 200 years until the fall of the city of Acre in 1291.

The Battle of Hattin

In 1187, the Muslim leader Saladin (1137–1193) lined up his army of 12,000 horsemen against 20,000 Crusader foot soldiers and 1,200 mounted knights. The battle was fought near two rocky peaks, called the Horns of Hattin, overlooking the Sea of Galilee. The Muslim forces surrounded the Crusaders, and after winning an outstanding victory, went on to recapture Jerusalem. This led directly to the Third Crusade.

French knight Baldwin (c. 1058–1118) is crowned King of Jerusalem on Christmas Day 1100.

The Ayyubid Dynasty

Saladin, who was of Kurdish descent, founded the Ayyubid Dynasty that ruled Egypt from 1171. By his great conquests over the Crusaders, Saladin expanded Ayyubid influence. After the great conqueror's death, his sons fought over the empire. But the dynasty remained strong until 1250, when the Mamelukes helped them defeat the Seventh Crusade and then took control themselves.

The castle called Krak des Chevaliers had two high walls and 13 towers. It held a garrison of 2,000 soldiers.

This 14th-century illustration shows Crusaders scaling the walls of a Muslim fortress.

The Kingdom of Jerusalem

After capturing Jerusalem in 1099, the Crusaders' leader Godfrey de Bouillon (c. 1058–1100) took over the city. Most Crusaders returned home, while those left defended Jerusalem. The following year, Godfrey's brother Baldwin became the first Crusader king of Jerusalem. Baldwin expanded the Kingdom's territory along the coast, and the rulers of the three other Crusader states became his vassals.

This ivory casket, dating from around 1200, was one of many treasures brought back from the Holy Land by Crusaders.

An image of Saladin engraved on a 13th-century silver vessel.

THE CRUSADER STATES

COUNTY OF EDESSA

KINGDOM OF ARMENIA

EDESSA

ANTIOCH

PRINCIPALITY OF ANTIOCH

KINGDOM OF CYPRUS

TRIPOLI

KRAK DE CHEVALIERS

COUNTY OF TRIPOLI

DAMASCUS

TYRE

Sea of Galilee

ACRE

MEDITERRANEAN SEA

KINGDOM OF JERUSALEM

JERUSALEM

EGYPT

PETRA

Crusader Castles
In order to defend the eastern frontiers of their states and to protect routes from the Mediterranean Sea, the Crusaders built strong castles. One of the most famous was Krak des Chevaliers (French-Arabic for "castle of the knights"). This mighty fortress was built on the site of a former Muslim stronghold that was captured by the Knights Hospitallers in 1142.

Crusader castle

Muslim castle

Crusader stronghold

Saladin used superior knowledge of the terrain to surround and overwhelm the Crusader force at the Horns of Hattin.

The wooden tower at the top of the mound was the strongest point of the early motte-and-bailey castle.

The Medieval Castle

Kings and nobles built castles as fortified strongholds where they were safe from their enemies. Medieval castles were so well defended that they were almost impossible to capture, except by a long siege to starve the occupants out. At the same time, the buildings acted as residences for noble families, knights, and servants. As well as places to eat and sleep, they included a chapel, a kitchen, and stables for the knights' horses.

Beaumaris Castle, begun in 1295 on the Welsh island of Anglesey, is a good example of a double-walled concentric castle.

The barbican was entered from the outside across a drawbridge over a ditch and through the outer gate.

Development of Castles

Early European castles were made up of a flat-topped mound, called a motte, which overlooked a fenced enclosure known as a bailey. In the 12th century, many wooden structures were replaced by a stone keep, or great tower. The keep was surrounded by a high stone wall, which provided strong defence. By the late 13th century, a second wall was added all the way around the castle.

A wooden drawbridge was lowered to allow people to cross the moat or ditch through the gatehouse. This was the castle's only entry point.

Strong Defences

Castles had a series of defences to keep out enemies. First, there was the ditch, which was often a deep moat filled with water. Then, there was a low stone wall, surrounding a higher, thicker wall with towers. Bowmen could shoot arrows at attackers through slits in the walls. The keep was the highest point and the most secure place in the castle.

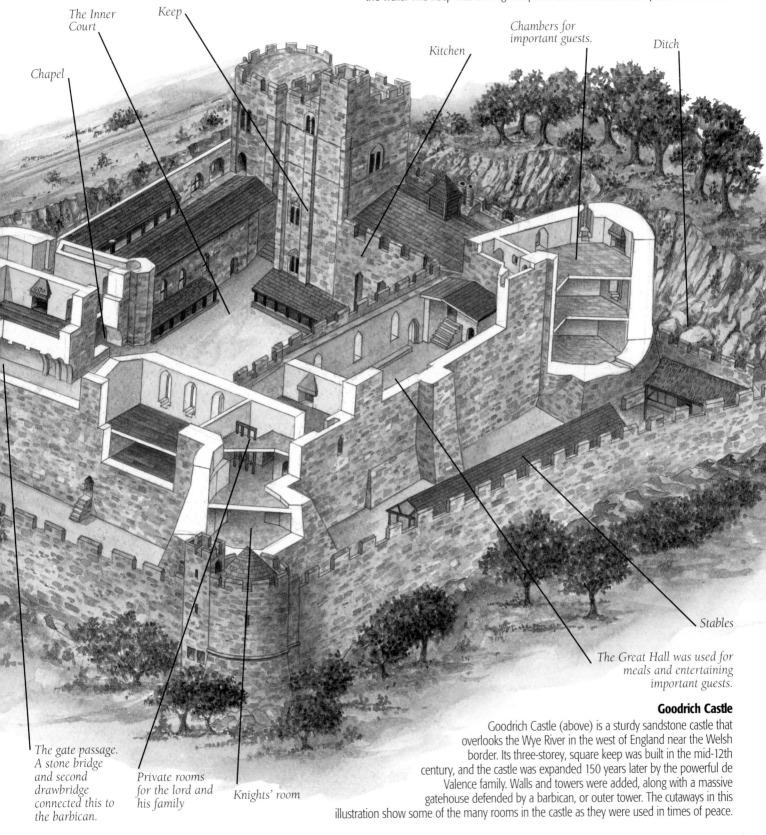

The Inner Court

Keep

Chapel

Kitchen

Chambers for important guests.

Ditch

Stables

The gate passage. A stone bridge and second drawbridge connected this to the barbican.

Private rooms for the lord and his family

Knights' room

The Great Hall was used for meals and entertaining important guests.

Goodrich Castle

Goodrich Castle (above) is a sturdy sandstone castle that overlooks the Wye River in the west of England near the Welsh border. Its three-storey, square keep was built in the mid-12th century, and the castle was expanded 150 years later by the powerful de Valence family. Walls and towers were added, along with a massive gatehouse defended by a barbican, or outer tower. The cutaways in this illustration show some of the many rooms in the castle as they were used in times of peace.

Inside Europe's Monasteries

In the late Middle Ages, many Christians led a religious life by joining like-minded people in groups that lived apart from the rest of the world. Monks lived in their own community in monasteries, and nuns in convents or nunneries. Different monastic orders followed the rules of their founders, and new orders were established and approved by the pope in the 12th and 13th centuries.

Daily Life
Life in the monastery or convent followed a regular pattern, with specific times set for prayer, study, and work. There were seven hours of prayer, beginning very early with matins (or morning service) and finishing in the evening with compline. The main meal was taken at midday, and study and work were fitted in between the hours of prayer. Work included growing vegetables, copying manuscripts, and caring for the sick.

These nuns are carrying music books on their way to Mass.

Monks and Nuns
The young men and women who took up monastic life knew that they would be cut off from the rest of the world. If they seemed suitable candidates, they became novices and trained for a year or more. Then, they took their vows and became full members of the monastic community.

The Monastery
The monks who lived in a monastery formed a self-contained community, separate from the outside world. The heart of the community was its church, or abbey, where prayers and services were held at set hours of the day and night. Other buildings surrounded the cloisters, which were covered walkways around a courtyard.

Dormitory

Cloister

Refectory

This 12th-century silver coin shows the abbess of a German convent.

Bell tower

Abbey or church

Monastic Vows

Monks and nuns lived by the rule, or set of guidelines, of their order. Many were based on the 6th-century rule of St. Benedict. In addition, all monks and nuns took three vows. The vow of poverty meant that they could not own any private possessions. Chastity required that they did not marry or have relations with the opposite sex. And a vow of obedience was made to the abbot in charge of the monastery.

In this 13th-century illustration, a novice monk receives his habit after taking his vows.

Infirmary

Kitchen

Abbot's house

Medieval Art

Romanesque and Gothic were styles of art that were popular in Medieval times. Most sculptures and paintings were commissioned by religious authorities and appeared in monasteries and churches. Their content was mainly Christian in nature, depicting saints and stories from the Bible. As styles developed, human figures became more realistic and elegant, leading towards the great artistic period of the Renaissance.

Painting for God

Romanesque churches were decorated with frescoes, or wall paintings, with subjects taken from the Bible. The Gothic style of painting was more naturalistic and elegant. By the early 14th century, paintings were growing in size and scale. Some of the best examples are altarpieces—ornamental panels that were placed behind the altar in important churches.

Right: A beautiful altarpiece in the Gothic style by Giovanni di Paolo (c. 1395–1482).

These sculpted reliefs stand beside the south porch at the Gothic cathedral at Bourges in France.

Romanesque Style

The style of art and architecture known as Romanesque was so called because it was based on the ancient Roman style. But it was influenced by other styles too, especially Byzantine. Romanesque was at its height between 1075 and 1125 in France, Italy, Germany and England. Its most important buildings were churches, which had curved (or "Roman") arches over windows, doors, and arcades.

A 12th-century Romanesque representation of the crucifixion from Spain.

This 15th-century limestone sculpture of the Virgin and Child was made for a Franciscan convent in France.

Sculpture Decorations

Romanesque buildings were decorated with relief sculpture carved from the stone background. From about 1150, the Gothic style took over. Human figures became longer and more graceful, and they were used to decorate doorways and large façades on the outside of cathedrals and other buildings. Gothic sculptors made greater use of detail, giving their figures individual faces and natural poses.

Tapestry as Art

Tapestry weaving required great skill. First an artist drew a sketch and worked it up to a full-scale pattern that a weaver could follow. The weaver then used woolen and linen threads of different colors to make up the picture. By the 14th century, Paris was the leading tapestry center. Most tapestries showed scenes from mythology or history. They were used as indoor wall-hangings.

This 15th-century tapestry of the Lady with the Unicorn was made in a style called millefleurs, which means "a thousand flowers."

A gold cup made in about 1375 for Charles V of France (reigned 1364–1380). Enamelled scenes tell the story of St. Agnes (c. 291–304).

Precious Metalwork

During the Romanesque period, the metal reliquaries that held the relics of saints became much larger, acting as shrines. Copper and bronze were used, as well as gold and silver, and glass-like colored enamel was added to metal vessels to give a smooth, glossy finish. Techniques were developed in the 13th century that allowed artists to pick out scenes in enamel.

One of 51 enamel plaques that make up the altarpiece at Klosterneuburg Abbey in Austria. It was completed in 1181 by master craftsman Nicholas of Verdun (1130–1205).

Building Cathedrals

Cathedrals were the most important architectural projects in the late Middle Ages. Some were originally built in the Romanesque style and then rebuilt, altered or extended in the Gothic style. Building often went on for centuries, as new decorations were added. Cathedrals were also lavishly furnished with works of art in the form of altarpieces, stained-glass windows, gold fixtures, and sculptures.

ARCHITECTURAL ELEMENTS

Arch
A curved structure spanning an opening. The Romanesque round arch is semicircular. The Gothic style introduced pointed arches.

Buttress
A support built against an outside wall. A flying buttress is an arched support that reaches from a column to the wall.

Façade
The front part of a building.

Pier
A solid support that is larger than a column (or round pillar).

Pinnacle
A slim, pointed tower typical of Gothic style.

Portal
A large, decorated entrance or doorway.

Rose Window
A circular window decorated with tracery (ornamental stonework).

Spire
A tower that narrows to a point at the highest part of a cathedral.

Vault
An arched roof. A barrel vault forms a single continuous arch. A groined vault is made up of two barrel vaults at right angles. A ribbed vault has projecting arches (or ribs).

Stained Glass

Many large Gothic windows were glazed with stained glass. The individual pieces of glass were colored with an enamel paint and framed by iron and tracery. The windows showed scenes from the Bible or the lives of saints. More than a hundred stained-glass windows were put in Chartres Cathedral in the 13th century.

This stained-glass window was made around 1200 for a Romanesque cathedral in Strasbourg, France.

Architects and Builders

Master masons were the architects of Medieval cathedrals. They planned the building, making simple drawings, and directed the building work. The stonework was carried out by hundreds of skilled masons, who used iron chisels and wooden mallets to cut and shape the stone, as well as carving decorations. Carpenters built scaffolding and a wooden framework for some of the building.

Builders at work at the base of a new cathedral.

The taller of the two spires dates from the 16th century.

The Romanesque Cathedral of Chartres in France was burned down in 1194. This illustration shows the Gothic cathedral that was built in just 25 years.

The stained-glass rose window on the façade dates from about 1210.

West façade escaped the fire. The round arches are Romanesque.

Above: The Romanesque cathedral at Pisa, Italy, was begun in 1063. The famous Leaning Tower is its bell tower.

Below: Parts of the Romanesque Basilica of St Madeleine at Vézelay, France, were later rebuilt in the Gothic style.

Building Styles

Romanesque churches had thick walls, rows of columns, round arches, and small windows. But the buildings were not all the same, and there were many regional styles throughout Europe. From about 1159, the Gothic style introduced taller walls, towers, pointed arches, and high windows decorated with stained glass.

Above: Durham Cathedral, England, built between 1093 and 1133, is a masterpiece of Gothic architecture.

This ornamental gargoyle projects from an exterior wall of the 13th-century Sainte-Chapelle in Paris. Gargoyles are water spouts that stop rain water running down the walls.

Ribbed vaulted roof

Gothic pinnacles

Flying buttresses support the weight of the vaulted roof.

Arch

The Royal Portal survives from the original Romanesque building.

Groined vault

Buttress

Trade, Merchants, and Bankers

Trading activity increased dramatically throughout Europe in the late Middle Ages. Passes across the Alps formed trading routes between Italian cities and northern Europe, and important sea routes connected the Mediterranean and North seas. Merchants formed themselves into guilds and traveled in groups for their own protection. Their trading successes helped those who produced raw materials, such as wool, as well as the craftsmen who turned them into finished products, such as clothing. Many bankers also became rich and powerful, as they financed long-distance trade and encouraged further growth.

Skilled craftsmen were needed to finish luxury products, such as this robe decorated with gold and jewels.

Making Cloth

Textiles formed the most important manufacturing industry. The best-quality wool was produced in England. Much of it was sold to the main wool-weaving centers of Flanders, such as Bruges. Flax was grown and woven into linen, and the finest quality was produced in Reims in France. All these textile products were sold to merchants, who traded them throughout Europe.

Merchants

By the 12th century, merchants were traveling long distances throughout Europe. Their most important goods were foodstuffs and textiles. They traded in wool from England, cloth from Flanders, salt and wine from France, and glass and other luxury items from Italy. By the 13th and 14th centuries, more people had the means to buy more goods. As demand increased, merchants grew rich and became important members of society.

Many different gold and silver coins were in circulation. They caused merchants problems and created a need for money-changers and banks.

This 14th-century illustration shows a wine merchant in Bologna.

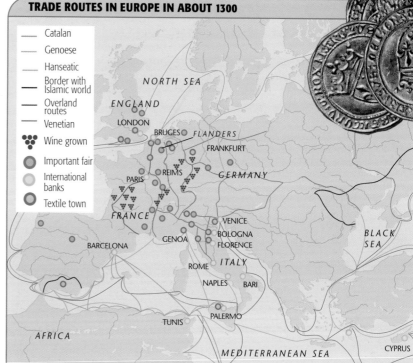

TRADE ROUTES IN EUROPE IN ABOUT 1300

- Catalan
- Genoese
- Hanseatic
- Border with Islamic world
- Overland routes
- Venetian
- Wine grown
- Important fair
- International banks
- Textile town

NORTH SEA
ENGLAND
LONDON
BRUGES FLANDERS
FRANKFURT
PARIS
REIMS
GERMANY
FRANCE
VENICE
GENOA
BOLOGNA
FLORENCE
BARCELONA
BLACK SEA
ROME ITALY
NAPLES BARI
PALERMO
TUNIS
AFRICA
MEDITERRANEAN SEA
CYPRUS

Trade in Medieval Europe

Long-distance sea trade was controlled by the city-states of Genoa and Venice. The Genoese traded around the Black Sea and opened a sea route from the Mediterranean to the North Sea. Venice mainly controlled the eastern routes. The Hanseatic League from north Germany traded across northern Europe, while the Catalan routes spread out from Barcelona across the Mediterranean. Merchants traded their goods at the seasonal fairs throughout Europe.

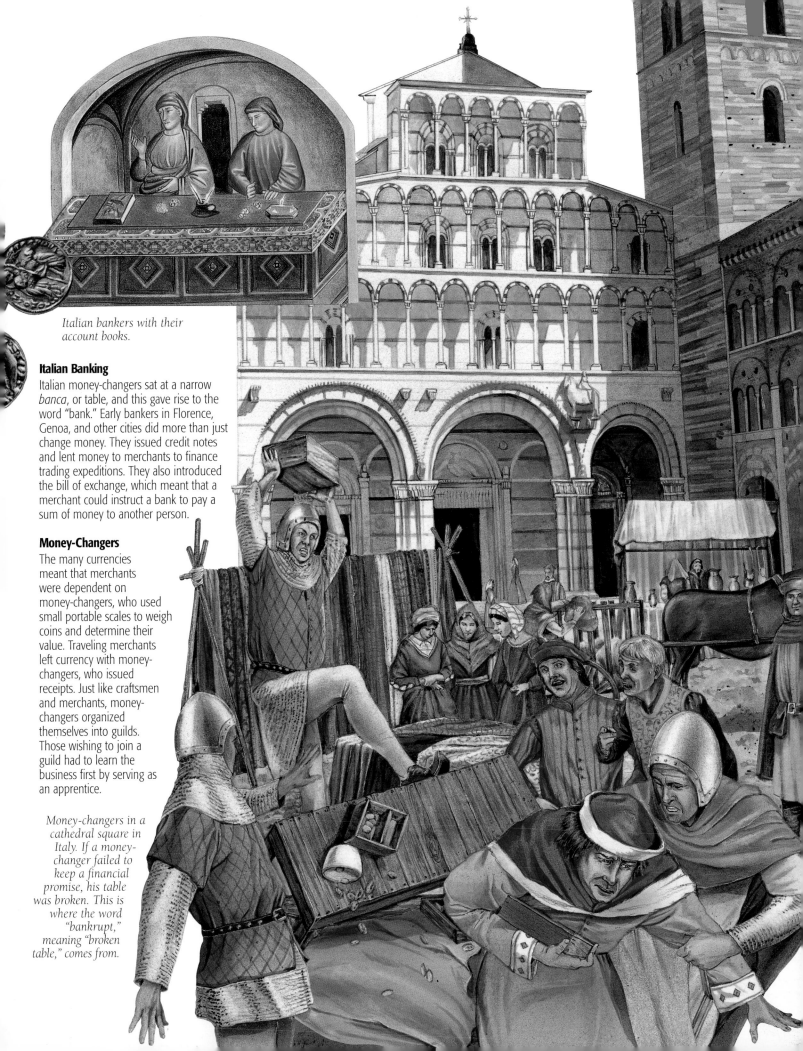

Italian bankers with their account books.

Italian Banking

Italian money-changers sat at a narrow *banca*, or table, and this gave rise to the word "bank." Early bankers in Florence, Genoa, and other cities did more than just change money. They issued credit notes and lent money to merchants to finance trading expeditions. They also introduced the bill of exchange, which meant that a merchant could instruct a bank to pay a sum of money to another person.

Money-Changers

The many currencies meant that merchants were dependent on money-changers, who used small portable scales to weigh coins and determine their value. Traveling merchants left currency with money-changers, who issued receipts. Just like craftsmen and merchants, money-changers organized themselves into guilds. Those wishing to join a guild had to learn the business first by serving as an apprentice.

Money-changers in a cathedral square in Italy. If a money-changer failed to keep a financial promise, his table was broken. This is where the word "bankrupt," meaning "broken table," comes from.

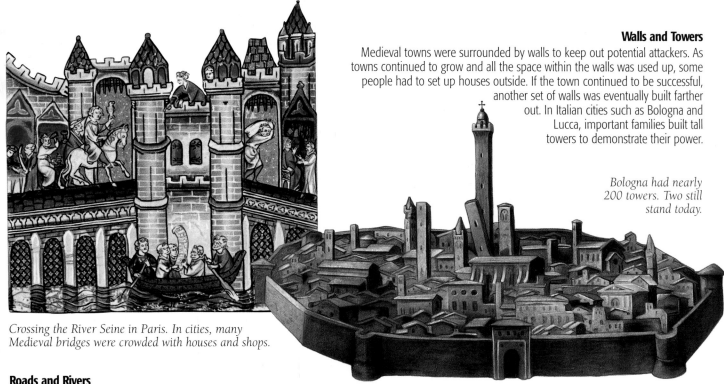

Walls and Towers

Medieval towns were surrounded by walls to keep out potential attackers. As towns continued to grow and all the space within the walls was used up, some people had to set up houses outside. If the town continued to be successful, another set of walls was eventually built farther out. In Italian cities such as Bologna and Lucca, important families built tall towers to demonstrate their power.

Bologna had nearly 200 towers. Two still stand today.

Crossing the River Seine in Paris. In cities, many Medieval bridges were crowded with houses and shops.

Roads and Rivers

Most towns grew up along the main trade routes of roads and rivers. A place where the two met and there was a ford, or later a bridge, was a natural location for a town. As their names suggest, Oxford and Cambridge are examples of Medieval towns that grew up beside convenient crossing points of rivers. Medieval builders were skilled in the art of building bridges of wood and stone.

Craftsmen receiving payment from officials for their work for the city of Siena.

Free Men and Women

There was a saying in the Middle Ages that "town air makes men free." This came about because former serfs had much more freedom in town than when they worked the land for the local lord of the manor. In many places, it was accepted that any serf who stayed in a town for a year and a day was free to practise a trade. He and his family then owed loyalty to the town council and the mayor rather than a lord.

The Growth of Towns

As Medieval towns grew in size and importance, they built high stone walls and gained independence from noblemen, bishops and kings. Conditions within towns were not comfortable, as streets were narrow and often full of rubbish. But people were attracted by the freedom of town life. Most moved there from the countryside to find work in the businesses of merchants, craftsmen, and shopkeepers.

Fairs and Markets

Many towns held an annual trade fair that lasted for several days. During the 13th century, fairs in the Champagne region of France became famous as the main places to buy and sell Flemish textiles and Asian spices. All towns had their own marketplace, where local people could buy and sell their produce. These were busy, noisy places. Traveling merchants were kept waiting before they could enter the market, allowing locals to do the best business.

The seal of the fortified town on Conwy on the coast of north Wales. The town was founded by King Edward I (reigned 1272–1307) in 1283.

Town Government

Towns became independent boroughs when they received a charter from the king or local lord. They were governed by a council and led by a mayor. The council was made up of leading burghers, who were usually successful merchants or craftsmen. In Italian cities such as Florence, powerful families vied with each other to gain control of local government.

This figure, painted in a fresco around 1340 called Allegory of Good Government, *represents the "common good" of Siena. The city declared itself an independent commune in 1167.*

A busy market scene beside London Bridge in the 15th-century. As England's main port, London was important to merchants from all over Europe.

Medieval Italy

The Italian peninsula was the scene of many different forms of government. In the northern region, powerful city-states, such as Florence, Milan, and Venice, relished their independence. They resisted control by the Holy Roman Emperor and the pope, who ruled his own Papal States. The southern half of the peninsula, including the island of Sicily, came under the control of the Normans, Angevins and other conquerors.

Southern Kingdoms

The Normans conquered Sicily during the 11th century and made the island part of a kingdom that included Naples and the southern part of the Italian peninsula. After King Roger II's death, his daughter married a Hohenstaufen prince, and Sicily came under the control of the Holy Roman Emperor. In 1266, Charles I (reigned 1266–1282) became the first Angevin king of the island. Angevin rule ended in 1282 when the Sicilians rebelled and massacred more than 3,000 French people living in Palermo.

Robert of Anjou is crowned King of Naples.

The tower of Siena's town hall overlooks the main square of the Piazza del Campo. Siena was governed successfully for many years by a council of nine burghers.

The octagonal Castel del Monte in southern Italy was built in 1240 for Emperor Frederick II.

Right: This detail from the Allegory of Good Government by Ambrogio Lorenzetti (c. 1290–1348) shows members of Siena's general council.

Northern City-States

The wealthy city-states were important centers of trade and banking. They grew rapidly during the 13th century, and their citizens' success and civic pride led to magnificent cathedrals, town halls, and other buildings being constructed. This development helped create the great cultural flowering of the Renaissance.

These copper horses were taken to Venice from Constantinople by Crusaders in the early 13th century.

ITALY

1060
Normans invade Sicily.

1130
Norman ruler Roger II becomes King of Sicily (reigned 1130–1154).

1198–1250
Holy Roman Emperor Frederick II rules Sicily.

1260
Ghibelline-controlled Siena defeats Guelph Florence at the Battle of Montaperti.

1277–1447
Rule of the Visconti family in Milan.

1282
The Sicilian Vespers uprising in Sicily ends French rule; Pedro III of Aragon (reigned 1282–1285) becomes king.

1288–1309
Building of the town hall in Siena.

1301
The poet Dante is forced to leave his native Florence by a group known as the Black Guelphs.

1309–1343
Rule of Robert of Anjou, "the Wise," over Naples.

Seals of the Ghibelline and Guelph groups.

ITALY IN ABOUT 1300

MILAN
VENICE
Po River
GENOA
BOLOGNA
RIMINI
PISA
FLORENCE
SIENA
PAPAL STATES
NAPLES
SARDINIA
KINGDOM OF SICILY
MEDITERRANEAN SEA PALERMO
SICILY

■ Part of the Holy Roman Empire
— Southern border of Papal States
● Republican commune
● Town under signorial control

Forms of Government

In the north, the Holy Roman Emperors mostly left the city-states alone. They governed themselves, either as communes (ruled by a council) or under a despotic ruler (signore). The Papal States controlled central Italy. The Kingdom of Sicily included the island and a large region around Naples.

Guelphs and Ghibellines

The names of the two most important political groups came from German (Welf, a family that controlled Bavaria, and Waiblingen, a Hohenstaufen castle). In the Italian city-states, people who supported the rule of the pope became Guelphs, while those who favored the power of the Holy Roman Emperor became Ghibellines. Rivalry between the groups was intense in Florence, where landowning nobles were Ghibellines and wealthy merchants were Guelphs.

Thomas Becket (c. 1118–1170), the Archbishop of Canterbury, was murdered by knights loyal to King Henry II of England (reigned 1154–1189).

England and France

The feudal system was particularly strong in England and France during the 12th and 13th centuries. At this time, kings were the head of government. In England, King John was forced to agree to a charter, and his need for support from important sections of society led to meetings that developed into the first real parliament.

The seal that King John of England (reigned 1199–1216) set to the Magna Carta.

Magna Carta

The Magna Carta, or "Great Charter," was presented to King John by a group of powerful barons at Runnymede. Its 63 clauses were based on the idea that a feudal lord, including the king, had obligations to his vassals, which in turn gave them certain rights. By agreeing to the charter, under great pressure, John confirmed that he was subject to the rule of law, just like all his subjects. This was important in the development of English constitutional law.

Edward's assembly of 1295 became known as the Model Parliament.

ENGLAND AND FRANCE IN THE 14TH CENTURY

The Angevin Empire
Henry II was the first Angevin ("of Anjou") king of England. In England, the dynasty of kings is known as Plantagenet (from the plante genêt or sprig of broom that Geoffrey of Anjou wore in his cap). Henry II was also Duke of Normandy through his mother, and he gained another province by his marriage to Eleanor of Aquitaine (c. 1122–1204). His son became Duke of Brittany, which gave the Angevins control over England and much of France.

Kingdom of England	Crown dominions
Border of English and French lands, 1154	Patrimony of the Count of Toulouse
French land ruled by England until 1154	Vassal territories
French from 1214	Imperial border
French land ruled by England until 1252	

SCOTLAND
YORK
ENGLAND
CAMBRIDGE
RUNNYMEDE
LONDON
CANTERBURY
FLANDERS
ROUEN
CHAMPAGNE
NORMANDY
BRITTANY
PARIS
ANJOU
BURGUNDY
AQUITAINE
FRANCE
BORDEAUX
LE PUY
AVIGNON
TOULOUSE
TOULOUSE
ARLES

English Parliament
The English parliament developed in the 13th century, when leading nobles and churchmen were summoned to advise the king. The assembly took more shape in 1295 when Edward I called on two knights from each county and two representatives from every town to attend. An important aim was to get agreement to new taxes so that the king could strengthen his army.

Richard II (reigned 1377–1399) clashed with the barons, who tried to use parliament to reduce his power.

Minstrels performed the works composed by troubadours. Most songs were on a romantic theme.

FEUDAL KINGDOMS

1128
Geoffrey of Anjou
(1113–1151) marries the
daughter of Henry I
of England (reigned
1100–1135); in 1154 their
son inherits the English
throne as Henry II.

1170
Thomas Becket
is murdered.

1214
Victory at the Battle of
Bouvines confirms Philip II
(reigned 1179–1223)
as ruler of northern
France and Flanders.

1215
King John seals the
Magna Carta.

1309–1377
Avignon in France serves
as home to the pope.

1314
At Bannockburn, Robert
Bruce of Scotland (reigned
1306–1329) defeats
Edward II of England
(reigned 1307–1327).

1381
English farm workers
march on London in the
Peasants' Revolt to protest
against
taxes.

Troubadours

Music and poetry were popular in Medieval Europe. In southern France, troubadours composed and sang in the Provençal language. Their favorite theme was courtly love, the chivalrous tradition of ideal love between a knight and a noblewoman. The poet-singers were called *trouvères* in northern France and *Minnesinger* in Germany.

Crusading King

Louis IX of France was one of the greatest Christian kings of the Middle Ages. He led two Crusades between 1248 and 1270. In the first, he was captured and held to ransom. The Eighth Crusade ended with his death in Carthage. He was declared a saint in 1297.

A 14th-century illustration of the death of Saint Louis IX.

The sceptre of King Charles V of France, who won back much of the territory that had been lost to the English.

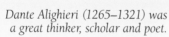

Engraving of King Arthur and his Knights of the Round Table.

Court Culture

The noble men and women who lived in the castles and manor houses of Medieval Europe had plenty of free time to enjoy pastimes and entertainments. At home there were banquets, while outdoors there were sports such as hunting and archery. Knights provided exciting, violent entertainment at tournaments, which were colorful pageants. From the 11th to the 14th centuries, Medieval literature developed from the epic romances and legends that had been passed down the generations.

Epics and Legends

France's greatest epic poem was the *Song of Roland*, which was written around 1100 by an unknown author. It tells the tale of a legendary knight who served King Charlemagne (reigned 768–814). In England, the popular legendary tales woven around King Arthur and his knights came from Celtic sources. Throughout Europe, epic romances were based on the heroic deeds and adventures of brave knights.

Dante Alighieri (1265–1321) was a great thinker, scholar and poet.

This metal plaque was attached to a huntsman's leather saddle.

French poet Christine de Pisan (1364–1431) presents her work to Queen Isabella of Bavaria (reigned 1385–1435).

Medieval Literature

Since paper was rare, Medieval authors wrote on parchment (dried, treated lambskin) or vellum (calfskin). Following the earlier romances, there was a burst of imaginative literature in the 13th and 14th centuries. Florentine poet Dante's *Divine Comedy* is a masterpiece of elegant literature and scholarly wisdom. It influenced the work of the later English poet Geoffrey Chaucer (c. 1340–1400), whose greatest work was *The Canterbury Tales*.

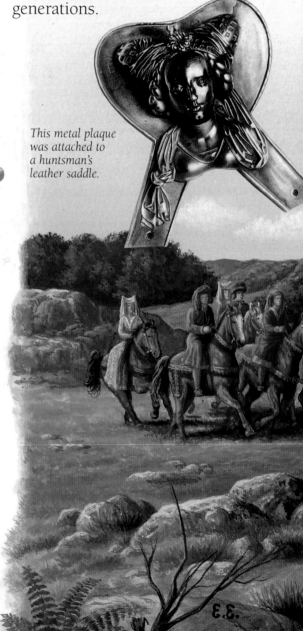

Great Banquets

Noble men and women held banquets to impress their guests with their wealth and generosity. Servants would bring several courses of meat dishes, as well as fish and poultry, followed by sweet puddings and candied fruits. The most important guests sat at a high table raised on a platform. During the feast, they were entertained by minstrels singing, playing music, and play-acting.

High table at a Medieval banquet.

Colorful Tournaments

The first tournaments were probably held in 11th-century France. These competitive festivals became very popular by the 13th century. They included jousts, in which opposing knights charged at each other on horseback and tried to unseat the opponent with a thrust of their lance. Ladies were able to watch their favorites in a spirit of courtly love and chivalry.

This ivory plaque, which served as the back of a mirror, shows ladies watching knights jousting.

Hunting as Sport

Hunting was very popular with noble families, serving both as an enjoyable pastime and as a form of military training. Noblemen rode through their own woodlands, chasing deer, wild boar, and foxes. They kept packs of hounds, as well as trained falcons and hawks, to help catch their prey. Horses called coursers were specially bred for hunting. Peasants were never allowed to hunt in privately owned woodlands. Successful hunts helped provide the ingredients for meat-filled banquets.

Lords and ladies enjoyed hunting on horseback. Small falcons called merlins were considered most suitable for huntswomen.

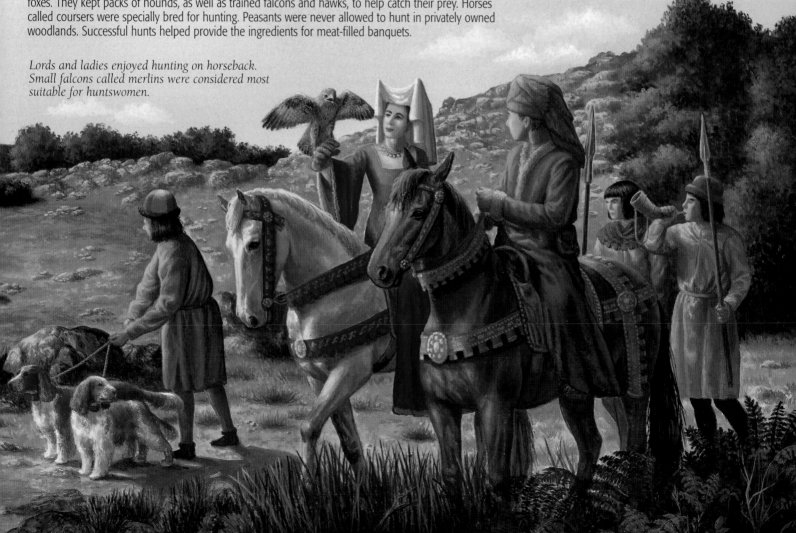

Germany and the Holy Roman Empire

T he Holy Roman Empire was a vast territory across western and central Europe that was ruled by German kings throughout the late Middle Ages. The relationship between this empire and the Church was a difficult one. Neither the emperor nor the pope wanted to give up overall authority, but they needed each other in order to rule all the people.

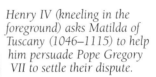

Henry IV (kneeling in the foreground) asks Matilda of Tuscany (1046–1115) to help him persuade Pope Gregory VII to settle their dispute.

A 13th-century image of Conrad III.

Investiture Dispute

A dispute between the German king and the pope began over the question of who had the authority to appoint bishops (known as "investiture"). Pope Gregory VII (reigned 1073–1085) fought with the German King Henry IV (reigned 1054–1106) over this issue. When Henry became Holy Roman Emperor in 1084, he captured Rome and replaced Gregory with Pope Clement III (reigned 1084–1100).

The Hohenstaufens

The Hohenstaufen family took its name from their castle at Staufen in Swabia. The family's founder was made Duke of Swabia by the Salian king Henry IV in 1079 as a reward for loyal service. In 1138, the founder's grandson took the German throne as Conrad III. His nephew, Frederick, succeeded him and became Holy Roman Emperor.

The Emperor's golden orb. Along with a crown, scepter, sword, and ring, this was a symbol of imperial power.

THE EMPIRE OF FREDERICK II

AACHEN · VERDUN · FRANCONIA · PRAGUE · SWABIA NUREMBURG BOHEMIA · ZURICH AUSTRIA · ARLES · BOLOGNA · FLORENCE · ROME · SICILY

Lands of the Holy Roman Empire

Frederick II was locked in a struggle for power with the pope. In 1240, after a successful victory over Italian communes, Frederick invaded the Papal States and threatened Rome. By then, he had already been excommunicated twice, and this happened for a third time in 1245. Frederick had been crowned King of Sicily as a boy, but a few years after his death, Sicily came under the rule of Charles of Anjou (reigned 1266–1282).

Kingdom of Germany	Added 1278
German lands owned by Hohenstaufen	Under Hohenstaufen control 1250
Kingdom of Italy	— Frontiers
Papal States 1178	— Frontier of Holy Roman Empire 1250
Added 1219	

Between Reigns

The period from 1250 to 1273 is known as the Great Interregnum (a period between reigns). This was a time of political disorder, when rivals for the throne put forward by the German princes had little power. Richard, Earl of Cornwall (1209–1272), was crowned king at Aachen in 1257, but soon after Alfonso X of Castile (reigned 1252–1284) was chosen by other electors. The princes finally chose a Habsburg, Rudolf I, as king.

Left: German princes deliberate on the election of their emperor.

Jan Hus

Emperor Charles IV was also King of Bohemia, and he made Prague the center of his empire. In 1409, the Bohemian religious reformer Jan Hus (c. 1369–1415) became rector of the University of Prague, which set him against many German teachers and students. As a critic of church practices, Hus was first excommunicated and then burned at the stake as a heretic.

Hus burned at the stake. His followers, known as Hussites, declared war on the Luxembourg emperor after his death. The Hussite wars, which sought to weaken German control in Bohemia, were unsuccessful.

Below: Jan Hus appeared before Sigismund, King of Hungary and Bohemia and Holy Roman Emperor (reigned 1433–1437). Sigismund approved the reformer's execution. Hus was condemned and a hat symbolic of heresy was placed on his head.

Medieval Spain

By the 11th century, the Moors, who had invaded the Spanish peninsula 300 years earlier, split their territory into small Muslim states. At the same time, the Christians of the northern region began expanding their kingdoms south. This *Reconquista* (meaning "reconquest") lasted from the 12th to the 15th centuries, when the separate Christian kingdoms were ready to unite Spain.

Spanish Kingdoms

During the period of reconquest, Spain was divided into separate Christian kingdoms. In the 12th century, Castile was the most powerful, and its ruler Alfonso VIII (reigned 1158–1214) tried to dominate his rivals in Aragon, León, and Navarre. He also tried to defeat the Muslims alone, but suffered a terrible defeat in 1195. This led to Castile joining with the other kingdoms to defeat the Almohad Moors in 1212.

A 12th-century portrait of Alfonso VII (reigned 1126–1157), the King of Castile and León who was crowned "emperor of all Spain."

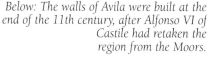

Wooden crucifix carried into battle by El Cid.

The peaceful Court of the Myrtles at Alhambra. The pool reflects light and enhances the geometric shapes of the Moorish architecture.

Muslim Influence

The Moors brought their advanced Islamic culture to the Spanish peninsula. They had made great discoveries in mathematics and medicine, and they made available many works of ancient Greek and Roman writers. The Muslims built beautiful mosques and fortified palaces in Spain, including the famous Alhambra fortress at Granada.

El Cid

Rodrigo Diaz de Vivar (c.1043–1099) was a popular hero who fought originally in the army of the King of Castile. He became known as El Cid, from Arabic meaning "the lord." When he was banished by Alfonso VI (reigned 1065–1109) after being wrongly accused of disloyalty, El Cid gathered his own small army. The army was hired by others and claimed many great victories.

CHRISTIANS AND MUSLIMS IN SPAIN

SANTIAGO DE COMPOSTELA
LEÓN
LEÓN
NAVARRE
PORTUGAL
ARAGON
CASTILE
COIMBRA
ÁVILA
TARRAGONA
TOLEDO
VALENCIA
CÓRDOBA
Las Navas de Tolosa
CÓRDOBA
MEDITERRANEAN SEA
SEVILLE
CÁDIZ
GRANADA
ALMERÍA

The Reconquista

By the middle of the 12th century, the whole of the northern half of the Spanish peninsula was back in Christian hands. The Battle of Las Navas de Tolosa was decisive for the reconquest, and this victory was quickly followed by others at Córdoba, Seville and Cádiz. By the end of the 13th century, only the kingdom of Granada was still in Muslim hands.

—— Frontier of Moorish kingdom (1146–1223)	→ Direction of Castile's conquests
—— Frontier of Moorish kingdom (1085)	→ Direction of Aragon's conquests
Christian reconquest of the 12th century	→ Direction of León's conquests
Christian reconquest of the 13th century	→ Direction of Navarre's conquests
Consolidated Christian territory, 11th century	→ Direction of Portugal's conquests
Last Muslim stronghold 1231–1492	⊗ Main battles
Land ruled by El Cid (1094–1102)	

Below: The walls of Avila were built at the end of the 11th century, after Alfonso VI of Castile had retaken the region from the Moors.

MEDIEVAL SPAIN

1085
Alfonso VI of Castile and
León recaptures Toledo
from the Moors.

1094
El Cid captures Valencia
and becomes the
city's ruler.

1146–1212
Almohads (from a Berber
tribe) control the Muslim
province of al-Andalus
(Andalusia).

1212
Alfonso VIII of Castile and
the armies of Aragon,
León and Navarre defeat
the Muslim Almohads at
the Battle of Las Navas
de Tolosa.

1238–1492
Nasrid Dynasty of
Muslims rules Granada
(and builds the Alhambra
palace on an ancient
fortress).

1262
Alfonso X of Castile and
León (reigned 1252–1284)
drives Moors out of Cádiz.

1478
Beginning of the
Spanish Inquisition.

1492
Conquest of Granada,
the last Muslim stronghold
in Spain.

Jews living in Spain had their own leaders who exercised authority over many aspects of life. This 13th-century Jewish Kashrut seal from Tarragona was used to designate foods that were fit for Jewish consumption.

Jewish Culture

During the Moorish occupation, Jewish people worked with many Muslim leaders as merchants and ambassadors. In the 10th century, Jewish writers in Spain began producing important works of philosophy and theology, and this led to a golden age of Hebrew literature, especially poetry. Jewish culture declined in the 12th century, and after the reconquest, Jews were required to convert to Christianity or leave Spain.

The Church and the Papacy

In Medieval Europe, the Christian Church was at the center of life. It was an authoritative institution, both rich and influential. The Church and its clergy were supported by kings and nobles, as well as by the practical contribution of peasants. There were power clashes between the head of the Church —the pope—and European rulers. Christian thinkers dominated the universities, and ordinary people were under great pressure to conform to the Church's doctrines.

This 14th-century painting shows St Thomas Aquinas receiving wisdom from evangelists and philosophers.

Study and Philosophy

Medieval Christian thinkers studied the works of ancient Greek philosophers such as Aristotle (384–322 BCE). By the 13th century, philosophy and theology were taught together at the developing universities. The German bishop Albertus Magnus taught this system of thought, called scholasticism, and his greatest pupil was St. Thomas Aquinas.

Mendicant Orders

The friars of some monastic orders (see page 18) depended on charity and lived by begging for alms. Four mendicant ("begging") orders were recognized by the pope in the early 13th century–the Augustinians, Carmelites, Dominicans, and Franciscans. Some other Christians opposed these orders as their influence grew, and in 1254 Pope Innocent IV (reigned 1243–1254) took away many of their privileges. Rights were returned by later popes, though smaller mendicant orders were suppressed in 1274.

This painting by Giotto de Bondone (c. 1267–1337) shows Pope Innocent III approving the rule of the mendicant order founded by Francis of Assisi in 1209.

Silver-gilt statue of the Virgin and Child. A strong cult of the Virgin Mary grew in the Middle Ages.

Heresy

The pope and his Church were determined to oppose heretics. They included anyone whose beliefs were different from the doctrines taught by Church leaders. In 1231, the pope brought in an official Inquisition, which led to violent methods of finding and dealing with heretics. Those convicted were told to change their views, but if they did not, they risked being burned at the stake.

This 15th-century Italian painting shows the devil trying to persuade a preacher to heresy.

The Great Schism

Pope Clement V (reigned 1305–1314) never set foot in Rome and moved the papal residence to Avignon in France. Efforts to return the papacy to Rome led to a split known as the Great Schism, when two rival popes were elected to succeed Gregory XI (reigned 1370–1378). Successors were chosen for both popes, until the dispute was settled in 1417.

The crowning of antipope Clement VII (reigned 1378–1394) by French cardinals.

Papal Power

Medieval popes built up great power and increasingly involved themselves in political affairs. During the 12th and 13th centuries there were constant struggles with kings and other rulers. In 1302, Boniface VIII went so far as to issue a decree stating that every human being's salvation depended upon submitting to the pope's authority.

A Medieval pope's gilt ring.

Marble statue of Pope Boniface VIII, from his tomb in Rome.

The Hundred Years' War

The long series of battles between England and France from 1337 to 1453 is called the Hundred Years' War. It covered the reigns of five English and five French kings, who struggled for control of France. The war began with great victories for the English, but by the end they were left only with Calais.

Edward III pays homage to Philip VI in 1330 for land held in fief from the French crown.

Battle of Crécy

The first major battle led to an overwhelming victory for the English archers, who defeated a larger army of mounted knights in northern France. More than a thousand French knights were killed, which was a severe loss. Edward III's 16-year-old son, Edward the Black Prince (1330–1376), commanded a wing of the English army and was the hero of the battle.

Build-Up to War

During the 1330s relations between England and France were not good. Edward III of England and Philip VI of France (reigned 1328–1350) were great rivals. They disputed the French crown, since Edward was the grandson of the former French king Philip IV (reigned 1285–1314). The two kings disputed land in the wine-making regions of southern France, and both wanted Flanders in the north, as this was the most important market for English wool.

English gold coin of 1344, on which Edward III (reigned 1327–1377) is shown aboard ship and described as King of England and France.

Above: A 14th-century illustration showing armed rioters ransacking the house of a wealthy merchant in Paris.

The Peasants' Revolt

In 1380, Richard II added a further tax to those already imposed on English peasants. Everyone on the tax register had to pay a fixed sum, which was needed to pay for the expensive military campaigns in France. This added to other grievances, and the peasants rebelled and marched on London. The king was forced to grant the people's demands, though he later withdrew the concessions.

Fighting at Crécy, where English bowmen and men-at-arms won the day.

In 1429, Joan of Arc accompanied her king to Reims Cathedral, where he was crowned.

Joan of Arc

When she was about 13, Joan of Arc (c. 1412–1431) believed she heard the voices of saints telling her to rescue France. She persuaded Charles VII, who was not recognized as king in northern France, to allow her to lead an army to win back the city of Orléans from the English. This victory meant that Charles VII could be crowned in Reims. In 1430, Joan was captured by the Burgundians and sold to the English, who burned her at the stake as a heretic.

Agincourt

The third famous English victory, following those at Crécy and Poitiers, was won at Agincourt near the coast of northern France. The English army, led by Henry V (reigned 1413–1422), was made up mostly of archers. It defeated the larger French army that engaged them on their way to Calais. Many noble French knights were killed, as Henry's reputation as king and commander soared.

Helmet of Charles VI, who ruled France from 1380 to 1422.

THE PLAGUE

A procession of flagellants takes to the streets.

There were three forms of plague:

Bubonic Plague
was the most common form. It is named after the symptoms of buboes (swellings in the armpits or groin); victims suffered severe headaches, fever, and vomiting; symptoms sometimes took days to appear.

Pneumonic Plague
affected the lungs, which became clogged up with a slimy substance red with blood; nine out of every ten victims died in a matter of days.

Septicaemic Plague
was the rarest form. It caused blood poisoning; victims suffered high fever and the skin turned deep purple (almost black, as in Black Death); victims died very quickly, usually the same day that symptoms appeared.

The Black Death

The plague known as the Black Death first spread from central Asia to the Genoese port of Kaffa on the Black Sea in 1346. Italian ships then carried the disease to Venice, Genoa, and many other ports. It soon traveled all around the Mediterranean Sea and took just a few years to reach as far north as Scandinavia. Death rates varied, but overall they were devastating.

Wrath of God

Many believed that the plague was a punishment sent by God in response to people's wickedness. Some tried to avoid this fate by praying for forgiveness and leading holier lives. In many parts of Europe, groups of people called flagellants wandered from town to town. They whipped themselves with spiked leather thongs to make amends for human sins.

This Medieval illustration shows the figure of Death strangling a plague victim.

This Medieval doctor is wearing protective clothing, including a beak containing spices.

The dead were carried away to be buried or burned. There were so many victims that many had to be buried in mass graves.

A detail from a 14th-century Italian painting shows the poor and the sick.

Spreading Infection

Many Medieval doctors thought that the disease was spread by bad odors in the air. In fact, it was caught from deadly bacteria passed on by fleas. The fleas picked up the bacteria from infected rats and then passed the disease on to any humans that they bit.

Plague Victims

The young, old, and sick were most at risk from the plague, but everyone was in danger of becoming a victim. The disease spread rapidly in towns and villages, where people lived closely together. Though they did not understand the causes of the plague, it seems that many did realise that they could catch it from infected people.

SPREAD OF THE BLACK DEATH ACROSS EUROPE

TRONDHEIM
BERGEN
OSLO
STOCKHOLM
REVAL
EDINBURGH
RIGA
DUBLIN
LÜBECK
DANZIG
LONDON
HAMBURG
SOUTHAMPTON
BRUGES
BORDEAUX
TANA
GENOA
VENICE
KAFFA
LISBON
MARSEILLE
TREBISONDA
VALENCIA
NAPLES
CONSTANTINOPLE
CÁDIZ
PALMA
PALERMO
ATHENS
TUNIS
ANTIOCH
SYRACUSE
HERAKLION

▨ 1346	▨ 1348	▨ 1350
▨ 1347	▨ 1349	▨ 1351

— Trade routes
— The Silk Route

The Spread of Death
Large numbers of villages were completely wiped out as the plague killed at least a third of the population of Europe. So many people died that population did not reach the pre-1348 level again until the 16th century. The map shows how the disease spread throughout the continent in just five years.

Fighting Disease
People believed that herbs such as rosemary helped to prevent bad air and therefore the spread of disease. For this reason, people held a pomander over their nose. They also tried potions of onion, peppermint, and treacle. Communities slowly began to realize that isolation helped stop the spread of plague, and in 1383, ships arriving at the port of Marseille were held in quarantine for 40 days.

Burying the dead.

Pomanders were filled with herbs and fragrances.

Infected rats spread the disease across oceans by traveling on ships.

Eastern Europe

Many regions of eastern Europe developed into kingdoms during the 11th and 12th centuries—Hungary in 1000, Poland in 1025, and Bohemia in 1158. During that period, Russia was made up of several powerful principalities. In the 13th century, these were invaded by Mongols, who made them part of their Khanate of the Golden Horde. During the late Middle Ages, the Baltic lands came under the power of the Teutonic Knights, until they were defeated by a united force of Poles and Lithuanians in 1410.

This icon of the Madonna and Child originated in Byzantium. It was taken to Vladimir in 1155 and then to Moscow in 1395 to help protect the city from the Mongols.

Religious Icons

The earliest Russian painters of religious art were trained by Greeks, who followed the Byzantine tradition of icons. These became the stylised holy pictures of the Eastern Orthodox Church. Icons were generally painted on wood, and the Russians added a number of saints to the list of those depicted, including Alexander Nevsky who was made a saint in 1547.

Russia

The cities of Kiev, Novgorod and Vladimir were powerful principalities in the 11th and 12th centuries. After the Mongol invasion, many Russians moved to Moscow, where Prince Ivan I (reigned 1328–1340) expanded the territory of Muscovy (the region around Moscow). Under Ivan the Great (reigned 1462–1505), Moscow conquered rivals Novgorod and Tver and became the most powerful city.

In 1242, the army of Alexander Nevsky, Prince of Novgorod (reigned 1236–1252), defeated a force of the Teutonic Knights on the frozen surface of Lake Peipus.

The castle at Marienburg was the seat of the Teutonic Knights.

A gold plate made for Conrad, ruler of the Polish duchy of Mazovia (reigned 1202–1247). Conrad invited the Teutonic Knights to subdue his Prussian neighbors.

THE BALTIC STATES FROM THE 12TH TO 15TH CENTURIES

NOVGOROD

NOVGOROD

Lake Peipus

RIGA

TEUTONIC ORDER

LITHUANIA

COPENHAGEN

BALTIC SEA

SMOLENSK

VILNA

HAMBURG

DANZIG

MARIENBURG

PRUSSIANS

Holy Roman Empire 1100

Frontier of Kievan Rus 1100

Eastern frontier of German settlement 1100

Possessions of Hungarian Angevins

Added to Holy Roman Empire by 1380

Frontier of German settlement 1400

BERLIN

WARSAW

NAUMBURG

POLAND

FRANKFURT

GERMANY

KIEV

BOHEMIA

VIENNA

HUNGARY

Expansion in the Baltic

From the 12th century, many German-speaking peasants moved eastward toward the Baltic Sea. Coastal towns, such as Danzig and Riga, became important trading centers. In the 13th century, Crusaders of the Teutonic Knights defended Polish territory against the pagan Prussians, and then took lands in Lithuania, Estonia, and Latvia. The early Medieval state of Rus was dominated by Kiev.

Poland

By the mid-12th century, Poland had been divided into many duchies and principalities. It was reunited in the 14th century by Casimir the Great and remained united under Louis of Hungary (reigned 1370–1382). Louis was succeeded by his two daughters. One ruled Hungary, the other, Jadwiga, ruled Poland. In 1386, Jadwiga married Grand Duke Jagiello of Lithuania (ruled 1377–1401), which united Poland and Lithuania.

Foreign Invasions

Early in the 13th century, Mongol horsemen swept into northeastern Europe from central Asia. They destroyed Russian cities, including Kiev in 1240, but allowed local princes to remain in power so long as they paid tribute. This situation lasted until the 15th century. In southeastern Europe, Serbia was attacked by Turks and became part of the Ottoman Empire. The Ottomans went on to capture Bulgaria and Greece.

In 1380, the Russian military hero Grand Duke Dimitri Donskoi (reigned 1359–1389) led his troops to a rare victory over the Mongols at Kulikovo.

A Mongol helmet.

Glossary

Agriculture Using land to grow crops and raise livestock.

Arcade Term used in architecture to describe a covered passageway with an arched roof.

Astronomer A scientist who studies the Sun, Moon and stars and other heavenly bodies.

Baron A nobleman or lord.

Caravan A group of people traveling together for safety, especially through the desert.

Celestial Term used to describe the heavens or the sky.

Ceremony A special event with particular rules done on special occasions, such as weddings.

Chivalrous Term used to describe the noble qualities that Medieval knights were supposed to have, such as courage, honor, and the protection of ladies of high rank.

Circulation The total number of all the coins of a particular currency being used at one time.

Community A group of people living in the same place, such as a monastery or town.

Concentric Term used to describe something that has the same center as something else. A concentric castle has two walls circling it.

Constitutional Term used to describe the laws and government of a country.

Corporation A group of people who obtain a charter giving the group certain legal rights and privileges.

Courtly Having manners fit for a court (the place where a king lives).

Cult Great admiration for a person, thing or idea.

Culture The shared customs, knowledge and behaviour of a group of people or civilization, especially in terms of the arts, such as music and literature.

Despotic Term used to describe someone who rules in a cruel and unjust manner.

Devastating Describes something that destroys and overwhelms.

Doctrines The religious teachings of the Catholic Church.

Dubbed Given the title of knight at a special ceremony.

Dynasty A line of rulers coming from the same family, or a period during which they reign.

Evangelist Someone who preaches the Gospel (the teachings of Jesus).

Excommunicate To take away membership of the Church as a punishment for wrongdoing. Only the pope had the power to excommunicate a king.

Fortified Describes a building that has been strengthened against attack.

Guild A union of people who work in the same craft or trade.

Heretic A person who holds beliefs that are contrary to those of the Church. In Medieval times, many people accused of heresy were excommunicated or burned at the stake.

Homage Showing honor or respect, especially to a king or other ruler.

Hospice A kind of inn where travelers can stop for rest and food.

Lease To let someone have land or other property for money (or other benefits) for a certain period of time.

Liberal A term used to describe something that is free and open to new ideas.

Logic The study of reasoning; a rational way of thinking about things.

Miracle An incredible event that seems to go against the laws of nature and science and is often thought to come from God.

Oath A promise in the name of God to do something, such as obey a king.

Order A group of monks or nuns who follow the rule of a particular founder, such as St. Francis of Assissi.

Pageant An elaborate show with lots of entertainment.

Papacy The position that the pope holds; also the length of time a pope reigns.

Pass A path cut through a mountain that allows people to travel from one side to the other.

Philosophy The study of human thought about the meaning of life and the correct way to live.

Principality A territory ruled by a prince.

Quarantine To isolate a person, animal, or thing from other people or animals for a period of time to prevent the spread of disease.

Rector The head of a school, college, or university.

Rhetoric The art of using words in speaking or writing so as to persuade or influence others.

Shrine A place of worship, usually with an altar or box containing a holy object, such as the bone of a saint.

Siege The surrounding of a city or fort by an enemy army in an attempt to capture it. A siege could last weeks or even months until the people inside were starving and forced to surrender.

Slavery The practice of owning people as slaves so that they have no rights or freedom and have to work for their owner.

State, the The government of a country ruled by a king or other non-religious leader.

Tax Money people must pay to a government, church or ruler to help support them or a particular cause.

Terrain An area of land, especially its natural features, such as rivers and mountains.

Theology The study of God and the religious beliefs of humans.

Whim A sudden wish or desire without any particular reason.

Index